Sailing to Freedom

by Jessica Gunderson

a Capstone company — publishers for children

Engage Literacy is published in the UK by Raintree.
Raintree is an imprint of Capstone Global Library Limited, a company incorporated in England and Wales having its registered office at 264 Banbury Road, Oxford, OX2 7DY – Registered company number: 6695582

www.raintree.co.uk

© 2018 by Raintree. All rights reserved. No part of this publication may be reproduced, stored in a retrieval system, or transmitted in any way or by any means, electronic, mechanical, photocopying, recording or otherwise, without the prior written permission of Capstone Global Library Limited.

Editorial credits
Jennifer Huston, Clare Lewis and Alesha Sullivan, editors; Kazuko Collins and Charmaine Whitman, designers; Eric Gohl, media researcher; Steve Walker, production specialist

Image credits
Capstone: 29, 33; Getty Images: Buyenlarge, 35, Historical, 53, Interim Archives, 49, PHAS, 44–45, Stringer/Hulton Archive, 22, Stringer/MPI, 39; Library of Congress: cover, 4, 8–9, 15, 27, 37, 43, 51 (all), 54, 56, 58; Naval History & Heritage Command: back cover, 30–31, 47; North Wind Picture Archives: 5, 7, 11, 13, 14, 17, 18–19, 21, 24–25; Shutterstock: Mybona, 41, scnhnc052008, 1, background (throughout)

Printed and bound in the United Kingdom.

Sailing to Freedom

ISBN: 978 1 4747 4591 8

Contents

Eleven kilometres 4

Born a slave 10

Working in Charleston 16

A daring plan 26

Sail to be free 36

Crossing Union lines 46

An American hero 50

    Timeline 60

    Glossary 63

    Index. 64

Eleven kilometres

Dawn crept over the horizon as a lone ship, the *Planter*, moved quietly through the waters of Charleston Harbour in South Carolina, USA. At the *helm*, Robert Smalls pulled his hat low over his forehead. The morning light in the sky worried him. He didn't want anyone to see his face and realize that he wasn't the ship's captain. His wife and children were huddled below deck, along with other people hoping to make it to freedom. The crew members moved around the ship. Smalls knew all their hopes were pinned on him to take them to safety. They had been slaves all their lives. Now freedom lay only 11 kilometres away.

Slavery and the Civil War

The year was 1862, and the United States was engaged in a Civil War. This was a war between the southern states and the northern states of the USA. The American Civil War had broken out in 1861, largely over the issue of *slavery*. Slavery had been used in the southern United States for hundreds of years. Black people were captured from the western coast of Africa and brought to the United States. Once in the USA, they were forced to work without pay and in terrible conditions. Enslaved people were bought and sold like property.

States in the South grew many crops. Cotton and rice were grown on large farms or plantations. Many slaves worked in the fields. Others worked in their owners' homes. Slaves had no legal rights and had to do whatever their owners asked.

After 1808, no new slaves were brought into the United States. But any person born into slavery remained a slave, with little hope of freedom.

Many people in the northern states thought it was wrong to use people as slaves. They wanted slavery to be *abolished*, or made illegal. But many people in the South felt slavery was important. They said they needed slaves to work on their farms. They wanted slavery to remain in their states and any new states that formed.

In 1860 some southern states decided to separate from the United States, or the Union. They formed their own country called the Confederate States of America, or the *Confederacy*. In 1861 war broke out between the Union and the Confederacy.

The War Between States

The Civil War lasted for four years. It was often called "The War Between the States" and involved much of the country.

More people lived in the North. The North also had more money, horses and railways. In many ways, it was more powerful than the South. But skilled soldiers in the South fought hard to protect their way of life. Battles were often long and hard. More men died in the Civil War than in any other American conflict.

FACT

About 620,000 soldiers died in the American Civil War. Not all died in battle. Many died from disease or lack of food.

Born a slave

Robert Smalls' story began many years before the Civil War. He was born in 1839 in Beaufort, South Carolina, USA.

His mother, Lydia, was a house slave for the McKee family. As a young child, she had been a field slave on the McKees' rice plantation on the Sea Islands, just off the coast of South Carolina. Working in the fields was backbreaking, tiring work. Slaves worked in the fields from dawn to dusk in the steamy heat. When they returned to their quarters in the evening, slaves often had even more work to do.

When she was 9 years old, Lydia was taken from her family and sent to the McKee home in Beaufort. There, she worked as a house slave and companion to the McKee children.

Lydia's later childhood was rather easy compared with other slaves, but she had been separated from her family at a young age. She understood how hard and cruel slavery could be.

FACT

Rice was a popular crop in coastal South Carolina. Slaves from rice-growing regions in West Africa were valued for their knowledge of how to grow rice and the way they could deal with the hot and humid South Carolina climate.

Born a slave

Because he was born into slavery, Smalls was the property of the McKee family, too. He began working as a slave when he was about six years old. His tasks were to brush the master's horses, row his fishing boat and carry his hunting bow. His master, Henry McKee, favoured him among other slave boys. The McKees treated Smalls well. His mother wanted to help him understand how brutal slavery was.

Lessons learned

Lydia took Smalls to witness a slave auction. Smalls watched as slaves, frightened and hopeless, stood on the auction block. White men inspected each slave to decide how much he or she was worth. Smalls saw husbands and wives sold to different masters and young children sold and separated from their parents. He began to realize the true horror of slavery.

His mother even took Smalls to see slaves being whipped and beaten. Smalls would never forget what he saw. He began to feel the need for himself and other slaves to be free.

Lydia also wanted Smalls to really experience the hard work that millions of slaves had to endure. She convinced McKee to let her son work in the rice fields. He worked from morning to night under the hot sun. This helped him to understand the hard work other slaves were forced to do.

"In law, the slave has no wife, no children, no country and no home."

—Frederick Douglass,
from a lecture on slavery,
1 December 1850

Smalls' fellow slaves told him about Frederick Douglass, an escaped slave who spoke out against slavery throughout the northern states. They quoted part of one of Douglass' speeches to Smalls: "In law, the slave has no wife, no children, no country and no home." Those words stayed in Smalls' mind. He wanted to become a free man, like Douglass.

Smalls learned that many young slaves had little comfort in their lives.

Working in Charleston

In 1851 the McKees sent 12-year-old Smalls to work in Charleston. Slave owners often allowed their slaves to work for other people in order to make more money. Because Smalls was strong and intelligent, McKee believed he would make more money in Charleston than he would as a field hand.

Smalls' first job was as a waiter at an exclusive restaurant in the Planters Hotel. He earned the equivalent of about £4 a month, but he didn't get to keep his earnings. Instead, he had to send the money back to the McKees.

While serving the restaurant's wealthy customers, Smalls often heard them discussing the benefits of slavery. Smalls didn't say a word, but he was angered by what he heard.

Six months later, Smalls got a job as a lamplighter. During the day, he went from corner to corner cleaning streetlamps. When darkness fell, he lit the lamps with a long candle.

On the docks

While living in Charleston, Smalls became interested in the city's waterfront. He loved to watch ships sail in and out of the harbour. When he wasn't working, he spent time on the docks, studying ships and talking to dock workers. He spoke with whites, slaves and black men who had bought their freedom. The people he met told him about "up north" where everyone was free. The idea of freedom did not seem possible to Smalls.

He remembered the horrors he'd witnessed at the slave auction and the whipping post. As he watched the ships sail into the horizon, he hoped that one day he would be free.

A new job

When Smalls had been in Charleston for about two years, McKee gave him permission to take a job working on the docks. First, Smalls became a *stevedore*, a worker who helps load and unload cargo, or goods, from ships. He was such a hard worker that after only a year, he was promoted to *foreman*. He supervised workers who were twice his age. He then made sails and became a *rigger* for a man called John Simmons.

Slaves loaded large bales of cotton onto ships.

Smalls wasn't content working on land. What he really wanted was to be able to sail on the water. Simmons was impressed with Smalls' skill and eagerness to learn, so he employed Smalls as a sailor to work onboard his coastal merchant vessel. This was a ship that sailed up and down the coast to deliver goods. Smalls quickly learned how to *navigate* and became a skilled sailor. Simmons promoted Smalls to wheelman, the term for a boat pilot.

Becoming an expert boat pilot

During this time, slaves were not allowed to learn how to read. Even though he couldn't read, Smalls spent a great deal of time studying maps and charts of the South Carolina coast. He soon knew every inlet, waterway and island in the area. He also studied water currents and tides, memorizing when currents shifted or when the tide came in and out. He sailed all along the South Carolina and Georgia coasts. His knowledge and skill made him one of the best boat pilots in Charleston.

Saving for the future

By this time, Smalls was earning about £13 a month. He gave his earnings to Henry McKee, who allowed him to keep roughly 80 pence. To earn a bit of extra money, Smalls used that 80 pence to buy fruits and vegetables from the islands he sailed to. Then he sold them to workers at the docks in Charleston when he returned. He saved some of his extra earnings and used the rest to buy more goods to sell.

Slaves were allowed to attend church. They could meet other slaves there.

Falling in love

When he was 16, Smalls met Hannah Jones, a slave of Samuel Kingsman. Kingsman hired Jones out as a hotel maid. Slaves who were hired out had more freedom to walk about town without someone watching their every move. As a result, Jones and Smalls were able to attend church together and go for walks along the waterfront.

Smalls wanted to marry Jones, but he also wanted them to live together as husband and wife. If slaves had different owners, they had to live with their owners, even after they were married. Smalls' and Jones' owners agreed to let them live together in a small apartment above a horse stable. They would still pay McKee £13 a month and Kingsman £4 a month from their earnings. Anything they earned above that amount, they could keep. The couple would use the extra money for food and other living expenses. It was not a usual way of doing things, but McKee and Kingsman agreed to it.

About a year after their marriage, the couple had a daughter, Elizabeth. When Smalls held Elizabeth for the first time, he looked down at her little face and a horrible thought came to him.

Smalls wanted his daughter to belong to him and his wife, not to the slave owner.

Because his wife was the property of Kingsman, his daughter was, too. Smalls realized that both his wife and daughter could be sold at any time, and he might never see them again. At that moment, he vowed to secure his family's freedom, no matter the cost.

A daring plan

After his daughter's birth, Smalls went to Samuel Kingsman to discuss how much it would cost to buy his wife and daughter. Kingsman agreed to a price of £640 for both. Although Smalls would still be a slave, his wife and daughter would belong to him. They could go with him wherever he went.

Smalls went on earning money by navigating the waterways and delivering goods to plantations along the Atlantic coast. At night, Hannah earned extra money by washing sailors' clothes and by working as a seamstress for the wealthy women of Charleston. After three years, they had saved £560. But times were changing in the nation then, and the country was on the brink of war.

War on the horizon

For years, northern and southern states had been arguing over the issue of slavery. Many in the North wanted slavery abolished. They thought it was wrong to use people as slaves, and they wanted the practice made illegal. But those in the South felt slavery was vital to their way of life. They wanted it to continue in their states and any new states that formed.

In November 1860, Abraham Lincoln was elected President of the United States. Lincoln was against slavery. He did not think slavery should spread to new states and the western frontier. His election angered and frightened many southerners.

President Abraham Lincoln

After Lincoln's election, many states in the South wanted to leave the Union and form their own country. They felt states should have the right to make their own laws, including laws about slavery. On 20 December South Carolina *seceded*, or split, from the Union. Six more southern states soon followed. These states called themselves the Confederate States of America.

President Lincoln wanted to keep the United States together. He didn't remove Union troops from Fort Sumter in Charleston Harbour, South Carolina. He believed South Carolina was still part of the United States.

On 12 April 1861, the Confederates fired upon Union troops at Fort Sumter. This was the first battle of the Civil War. The Union lost the battle, and later a total of 11 states joined the Confederacy. After the battle at Fort Sumter, more battles broke out. The nation was engaged in a full-on war between the Union and the Confederacy.

The war caused feelings of both hope and dread for Smalls. If the North won the war, he and all the other slaves in the South could be freed from slavery. But if the South won, slavery could carry on for years to come.

When Hannah gave birth to a son in 1861, Smalls was overjoyed but worried. Another child meant he would have to save even more money to purchase his family's freedom. He began to think about an escape plan.

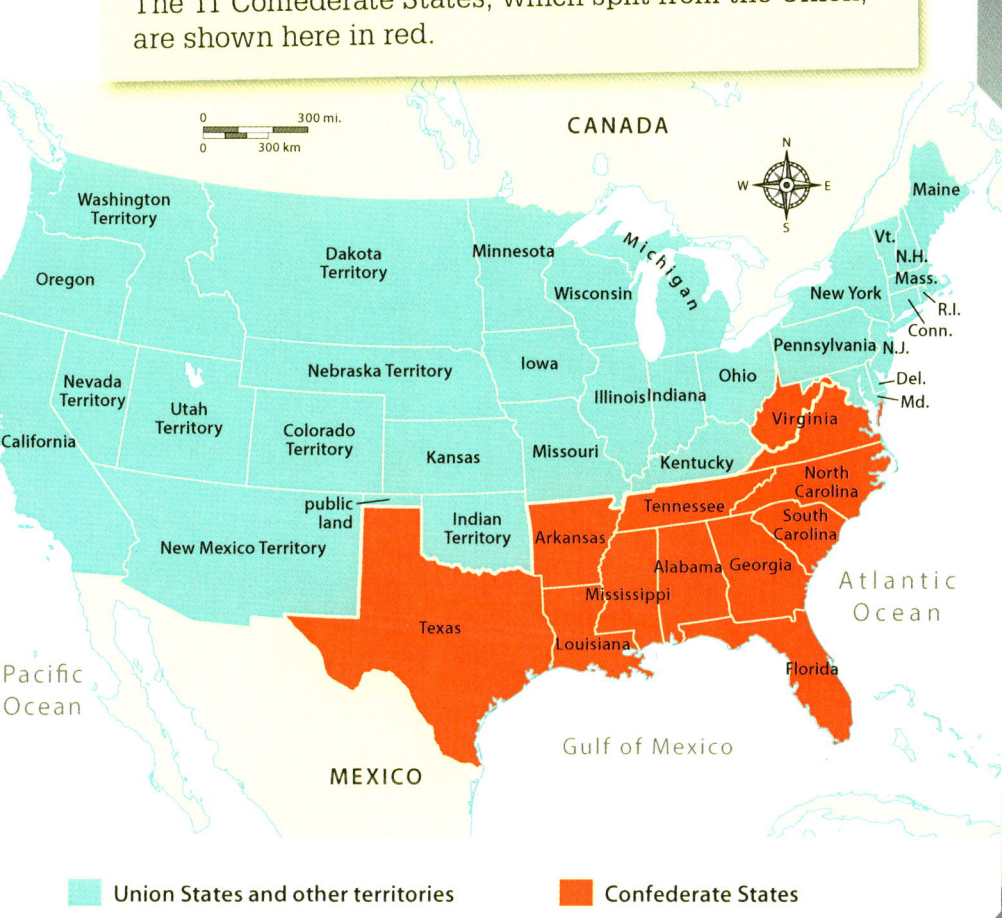

The 11 Confederate States, which split from the Union, are shown here in red.

Working for the enemy

Before the war broke out, Smalls had been working for John Ferguson on the *Planter*. This large, 14-metre steamer had been designed to carry cotton from plantations to be sold. Once the war began, Ferguson rented the *Planter* and its slave crew members to the Confederacy. Because Smalls was part of the deal, he had no choice but to work on the ship for the Confederacy.

The *Planter* carried two cannons, so it became a useful Confederate war vessel. It was large enough to transport 1,000 troops along with their weapons and could also sail on South Carolina's rivers.

Due to Smalls' earlier work and his knowledge of the bays of the area, the Confederate officers made him a wheelman. In this role, Smalls steered the boat and learned the secret whistle codes that allowed the *Planter* to pass Confederate forts located along the Atlantic coast. The *Planter* patrolled Charleston Harbour, planting mines, laying torpedoes and carrying Confederate troops and weapons to these nearby forts.

The *Planter* is shown here in the 1860s. The ship is loaded with cotton.

Union troops capture Port Royal

In late 1861, Union forces captured the towns of Port Royal and Beaufort, just down the coast from Charleston. Smalls received word that his mother, Lydia, had been living in Port Royal when the town was captured. She was working as a cook for Major General David Hunter, a Union officer. Hunter wanted to give Lydia and all other Port Royal slaves their freedom. Now that his mother was close to being free, Smalls was even more eager to secure freedom for the rest of his family.

Blockade!

After the capture of Port Royal, the Union Navy set up a *blockade* of Charleston Harbour. This blockade prevented Confederate ships from sailing out into the Atlantic Ocean and also stopped supplies from coming in. The blockade almost cut off Charleston's harbour and its forts.

The grey arrows show the journey taken by Smalls in the *Planter*.

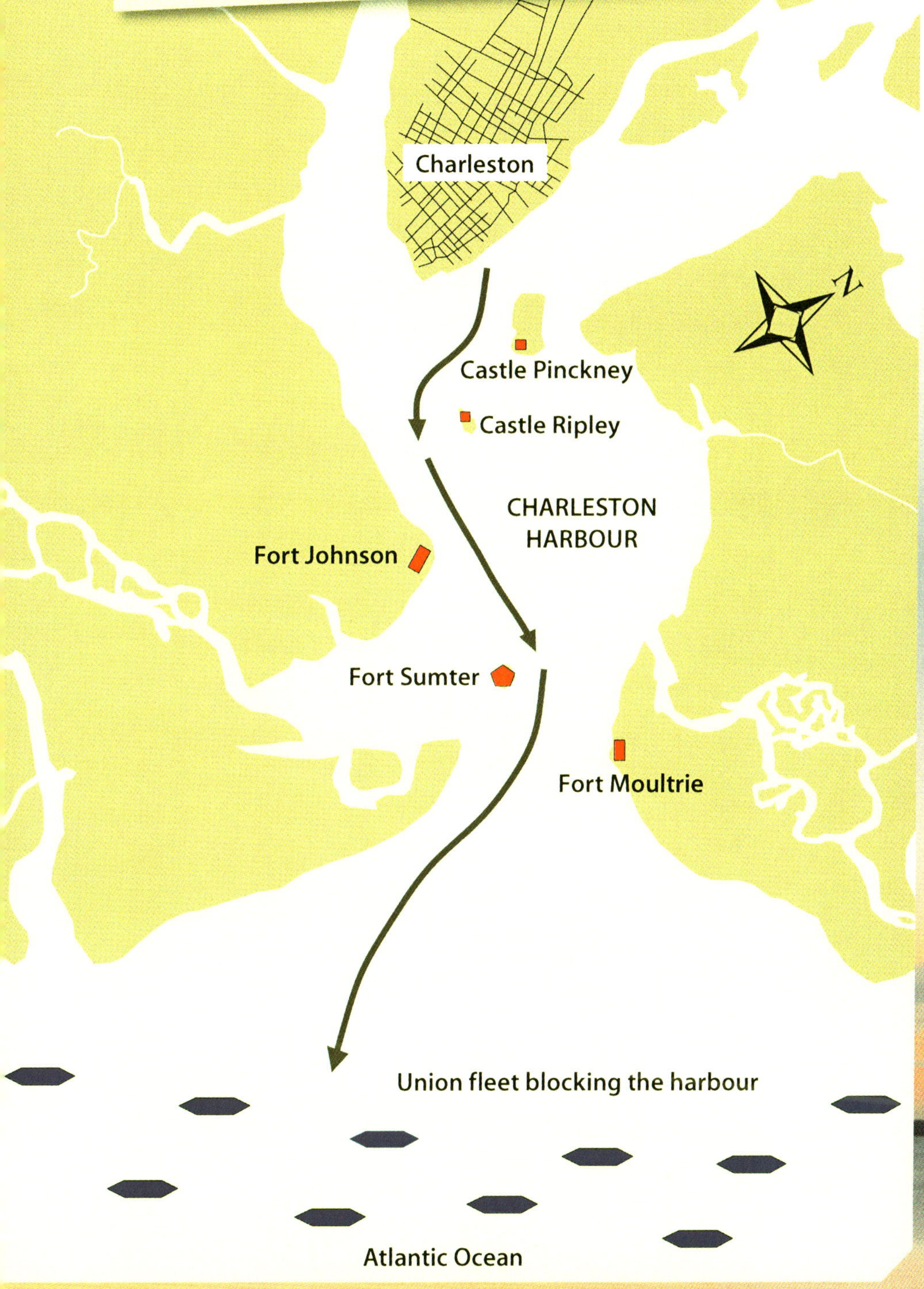

Charleston

Castle Pinckney

Castle Ripley

Fort Johnson

CHARLESTON HARBOUR

Fort Sumter

Fort Moultrie

Union fleet blocking the harbour

Atlantic Ocean

33

Confederate ships could still deliver troops and supplies to forts within the harbour or inland along rivers and channels. The *Planter* stayed in Charleston Harbour as a guard boat and supply vessel. From his pilot's post on the *Planter* in Charleston Harbour, Smalls could peer through the captain's binoculars and see the Union fleet anchored 11 kilometres away.

A joke turns into an escape plan

One day, when the *Planter*'s white officers had gone ashore for the night, Smalls was joking around with his fellow crew members, all of whom were slaves. He put on the captain's wide straw hat and stood at the wheel. One of the crew members told Smalls that he could pass for CJ Relyea, the *Planter*'s captain.

The crewmate's words sparked an idea in Smalls. He looked towards the horizon where he could see the Union fleet just a few kilometres away. A daring plan began to take shape in his mind.

Union sailors on the deck of USS *New Hampshire*, off Charleston, South Carolina, around 1864.

Sail to be free

One Sunday in April 1862, the *Planter*'s black crew members gathered in the Smalls' tiny apartment on East Bay Street in Charleston. They had come to listen to Smalls' plan. Smalls explained that the *Planter*'s officers often spent nights on shore, even though it was against orders. While they were ashore, Smalls and his crewmates could steal the *Planter*. They would then pick up their wives and children and sail to Union-held waters and freedom. But they would have to be ready at a moment's notice. And if they were caught, they could be badly beaten, imprisoned or even put to death.

One by one, the crew members agreed to the plan. They also decided that if they were caught, they would fight to the death and sink the ship rather than return to a life of slavery.

Hannah was aware of the plan, too. When she received word, she would sneak away from their home with their children. They would go to a merchant ship called the *Etowah* that was docked in Charleston Harbour. Two slave crew members of the *Etowah* were in on the plan. There, Hannah and the children would wait.

Hannah knew that if the plan failed, she and her children would probably face death. But a future of freedom was worth the risk, so she agreed.

the *Planter*

The moment of truth arrives

Now, Smalls just needed to find the right moment for escape. On 12 May 1862, that moment finally arrived.

That day, the *Planter*'s crew was loading the ship with six heavy guns and 200 rounds of ammunition. One of the heavy guns was a cannon that had been taken from Fort Sumter after the Union surrendered. The guns and ammunition were to be delivered to Confederate forts around Charleston Harbour. After this, the white officers planned to spend the night on shore.

This painting shows slaves moving a cannon in Charleston.

Smalls thought to himself that the weapons would be a great gift to the Union forces. He whispered to his fellow slaves to slow down the loading process so the cargo couldn't be delivered that day. So the crew worked slowly on purpose. By nightfall, the weapons had been loaded, but the journey to deliver them would have to wait until morning. As the white officers walked down the *gangplank* to spend the night on shore, the captain told Smalls to be ready to set sail at 6am.

Once the officers were safely on shore, Smalls and the other crew members sprang into action. They sent word to their wives to head to the *Etowah*. Then they set about stacking wood to fire up the steam engine's *boilers*. Smalls crept into the captain's quarters and slipped into a white shirt, jacket and the captain's wide-brimmed straw hat. Then he took his place at the wheel. The moment had finally arrived!

At about 3am, the *Planter*'s engines roared to life. The sound echoed throughout the silent harbour. Smoke from the engines wafted towards the city. Smalls watched the smoke and hoped no one in Charleston would see it and sound a fire alarm.

The escape begins

Smalls called to the men to raise the Confederate and South Carolina flags. Then he blew the whistle to signal that the ship was leaving. As he guided the boat away from the dock, Smalls scanned the dark waterfront. He hoped the guards who patrolled the *wharf* would not suspect anything. The guards did notice the ship leaving early, but no one raised an alarm.

With the Confederate flag flying high on the ship, Smalls hoped to pass the forts safely.

FACT

Two slave crew members did not join the escape because they were afraid of what might happen to their families. They stayed behind and, when questioned, said they knew nothing of the plan.

On the *Etowah*, Hannah held her children close and waited. With her were four other women and another child, the families of the other crew members. Hannah stared at the dark horizon. When she caught sight of the *Planter*, she let out a sigh of relief. The escape to freedom was about to begin.

A *Planter* crewman hopped into a rowing boat and rowed towards the wharf to retrieve the waiting families as well as three other slave men. When they'd climbed aboard the rowing boat, he swiftly rowed back to the *Planter*. Day would break soon. They had no time to lose.

Once aboard, the women and children were led to the hold below deck. Smalls then steered the ship towards the mouth of the harbour, where the Union blockade stood. Then the most dangerous part of the escape began. The *Planter* would have to pass a few heavily armed Confederate forts. At each fort, lookouts scanned the waters for possible attack and cannons stood ready to fire. Fort Sumter would be the biggest obstacle of all. This main Confederate fort near the mouth of the harbour was a heavily guarded fortress. It had high stone walls, loaded cannons and watchful guards. If caught, the *Planter*'s crew and families would be in great danger.

Fooling the guards

As the *Planter* neared the first Confederate fort, Castle Pinckney, Smalls sounded the secret signal to request passage. He'd passed the post many times before, and this time was no different. No alarms sounded. No shots rang out. Smalls kept the ship at a slow speed so not to look suspicious as he sailed the ship seaward. He safely passed the next two forts, Fort Ripley and Fort Johnson, at the same slow pace. And then he saw Fort Sumter looming ahead.

Fort Johnson with Fort Sumter in the distance

Dawn was starting to break. Rays of light peeked across the eastern horizon. Passing the fort would be even more dangerous in the daylight. Smalls pulled his hat down lower over his brow. He folded his arms in the same way Captain Relyea did. He glanced up to make sure the Confederate flag was still flying high. Then he sounded the secret signal to pass – two long whistles and one short blast.

Fort Sumter

Time seemed to stand still. It seemed like forever until the Fort Sumter guard waved at the *Planter*, giving the OK to pass. Smalls moved the ship forwards, gliding directly below the fort's guns. At that moment, he prayed to God to stand guard over himself and his family and guide them to their promised land of freedom.

Crossing Union lines

Smalls maintained a steady pace past Fort Sumter. Once the *Planter* was out of range of Fort Sumter's guns, he lunged the ship forwards at full speed, racing towards Union waters.

The lookout on Fort Sumter saw the *Planter* speeding towards the Union fleet and realized something was wrong. He sounded the alarm, but it was too late. The *Planter* was too far away to catch or shoot. Even so, the 17 slaves – nine men, five women and three children – on the ship weren't safe yet. They still had to make it to the Union fleet.

Aboard the ship, Smalls could see the Union ships shining in the early morning light. "Lower the flags!" he ordered.

Once the Confederate and South Carolina flags were lowered, a white bedsheet was raised in surrender. Smalls hoped the Union soldiers would see the white flag and know not to fire. He steered the *Planter* towards the *Onward*, one of the Union fleet's gunboats.

> "...please stand guard over us and guide us to our promised land of freedom."
>
> —Robert Smalls

Smalls steered the ship towards the Union fleet.

Prepare to fire!

From the *crow's nest* of the *Onward*, the lookout saw the *Planter* charging towards them at full speed. He shouted an alert to the captain, JF Nichols.

Nichols took one look at the *Planter* and thought that the Union fleet was under attack. He turned the *Onward* to face the *Planter* and told his men to prepare to fire their cannons.

Seeing the guns pointed right at the *Planter*, Smalls swung the boat around. The white flag flapped in the wind. Aboard the *Onward*, a Union sailor told the captain that he could see a white flag.

Nichols ordered his crew to hold their fire. As the *Planter* steamed closer, he signalled for the boat to pull alongside the *Onward*. Nichols was amazed at what he saw – an entirely black crew sailing a Confederate warship bravely towards him.

Freedom at last

As the *Planter* coasted up to the *Onward*, Smalls leaned against the railing and waved to Nichols. The captain stepped onto the *Planter*'s deck and was surrounded by joyous cheers.

Robert Smalls (top) and some of the other men who escaped on the *Planter*.

Smalls took off his hat in welcome and said, "Good morning, sir! I've brought you some of the old United States guns, sir!"

The *Planter*'s crew began cheering wildly. They knew they'd made it to freedom.

As Captain Nichols raised the American flag on the *Planter*'s mast, the crew cheered again. Hannah and the other women and children emerged from the hold to see the flag – a symbol of freedom – flying high above them.

An American hero

In Charleston, Confederate General RS Ripley woke to the news that the *Planter* had disappeared. The troops who had guarded the *Planter* that night said they'd seen who they thought was the captain in the pilothouse. After all, he was wearing captain's clothes and a straw hat, just like Captain Relyea. And because they knew the ship was to depart early, they didn't sound an alert.

General Ripley – unable to believe that slaves had stolen the ship – gazed off into the distance to see the *Planter* at the mouth of the harbour. It was secured between Union warships. He wanted the *Planter*'s officers to be punished because they had left their post on the ship to spend the night on shore. The officers were found guilty but were later released.

Safely in Union hands, the *Planter* – along with Smalls and his crew – sailed to Union headquarters on Port Royal. There, Smalls told Admiral Samuel DuPont the story of their escape. He also gave DuPont a logbook from the ship, which revealed Confederate codes and secret signals.

Smalls' knowledge of Charleston Harbor proved vital to the Union as well. He was able to tell the Admiral the exact locations of the Confederate forts and the mines and torpedoes they had hidden.

For the capture of guns, ammunition and a warship, the US government gave Smalls a reward of £1,200. Other members of his crew received smaller rewards as well.

A valuable gift

The *Planter* proved to be valuable to the Union forces. Because it was a shallow-water ship, it could navigate the rivers of coastal South Carolina with ease. DuPont asked Smalls to remain as pilot of the *Planter*. But because of a rule that required navy pilots to be able to read and write, Smalls could not join the Union navy. Instead, he joined the Union army, which then loaned him to the navy. Later in the war, President Lincoln reversed the rule that pilots had to be able to read and write. In December 1863, Smalls was promoted, making him the first black captain of the US Navy.

Robert Smalls as a free man

FACT

A newspaper in New York wrote about Smalls' journey to freedom as one of the most daring adventures of the American Civil War.

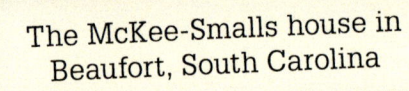

The McKee-Smalls house in Beaufort, South Carolina

FACT

After McKee died, Smalls moved McKee's widow, Jane, into the Smalls' house. He took care of her until she died in 1904.

Because of his heroic deed, Smalls was granted a meeting with President Lincoln. During that meeting, Smalls convinced the president to allow African-Americans to serve in the Union Army. For that reason, Smalls is praised for his role in recruiting 5,000 black soldiers to fight for the Union.

Going home

Hannah and their children were sent to Beaufort, where they would be safe because the area was under Union control. In 1863 Smalls learned that the former McKee home in Beaufort had been left by its new owners when the Union took over the town. The owners didn't pay taxes on the house, so the US government put it up for sale. With part of his reward money, Smalls purchased the home where he had once served as a slave.

After the war, the McKees were left without a home and nearly penniless. Smalls, on the other hand, was in a position to return the kindness the McKees had shown him and his mother when he was a child. Smalls bought a home for the McKees and drove them around town in his carriage. Henry McKee – his former master – died in 1875.

A hero to some, a traitor to others

Northerners thought of Smalls as a hero and a symbol of the strength and courage of the African-American people. But Southerners viewed him as a traitor and offered a £3,000 reward for his capture. Despite this *bounty* on his head, Smalls served the Union for the rest of the war. He fought in a total of 17 naval battles. He also gave speeches against slavery.

Philadelphia in the late 1800s

A natural-born leader

Smalls spent some time in Philadelphia in 1864, while waiting for repairs to be finished on the *Planter*. During this time, Smalls started learning to read and write and also gave speeches to the Anti-Slavery Society. But it was also during this time that Smalls was told to give up his seat on a streetcar to a white person. The driver told him to stand on the outside platform in the rain instead.

Insulted by this racial injustice, Smalls walked home in the rain. Many people were outraged by this unfair treatment of a national hero. A mass protest followed the event. Smalls took part in the protest. In 1867, Philadelphia changed the laws on *segregation* on public transportation. All people, whatever their race, could sit anywhere they wanted.

After the Union won the war in 1865, Smalls returned to Beaufort, South Carolina. Although the war was over and slavery had ended, Smalls never stopped fighting for his fellow African-Americans. Believing strongly in the importance of education, he opened a school for black children in Beaufort in 1867.

Smalls later served in the South Carolina state legislature, where he pushed for equal rights for African-Americans. In 1874, he was elected to the US Congress as a Representative of South Carolina. During his five terms in office, he worked for the rights of African-Americans and women. He believed in equal rights for all. In 1895, South Carolina leaders met to draft a new state constitution that would deny African-Americans equal rights. Smalls went to the meeting and spoke out against the new laws. But the laws were passed, taking away the right to vote for almost all black people in South Carolina.

A lifelong freedom fighter

After a long life of fighting for equality and freedom for his people, Smalls died in 1915. In 2007 the US Army named one of its ships the *USAV Major General Robert Smalls*. It was the first army vessel named after an African-American.

A statue near Smalls' grave in Beaufort is engraved with his words from the 1895 constitutional convention: "My race needs no special defence, for the past history of them in this country proves them to be the equal of any people anywhere. All they need is an equal chance in the battle of life."

Timeline

1839 — Robert Smalls is born on 5 April in McKee slave quarters in Beaufort, South Carolina, USA.

1851 — Smalls is sent to Charleston to work as a hired-out slave.

1856 — Smalls marries Hannah Jones, a slave working as a hotel maid.

1858 — The Smalls' daughter Elizabeth is born.

1861 — Smalls begins working on the *Planter*. His son Robert Jr is born. On 12 April, the American Civil War begins with the Battle of Fort Sumter.

1862 — In the early hours of 13 May, Smalls steers the *Planter* across Union lines, freeing himself as well as 16 other slaves.

1863	Smalls buys the old McKee home in Beaufort, where he had been born a slave. His son, Robert Jr, dies of whooping cough, and their second daughter, Sarah, is born.
1864	In late December, Smalls is told to give up his seat on a streetcar in Philadelphia.
1867	Smalls joins other black people to form the Beaufort County School Board and opens a school for black children.
1868	Smalls helps write the South Carolina state constitution.
1868–1870	Smalls serves a term in the South Carolina State House of Representatives.
1870–1874	Smalls serves in the South Carolina State Senate.
1872	Smalls begins leading a newspaper in Beaufort called the *Southern Standard*.

Timeline (CONTINUED)

1875–1887   Smalls serves five terms in the US House of Representatives.

1883   Smalls' wife Hannah dies.

1890   Smalls marries Annie Wigg.

1892   Smalls and Annie have a son, William.

1895   Smalls' wife Annie dies. Smalls speaks out against the rewriting of the South Carolina state constitution.

1915   Smalls dies at his home on Prince Street in Beaufort.

Glossary

abolish put an end to something

blockade closing off of an area to stop people or supplies going in or out

boiler tank that boils water to produce steam

bounty reward or money offered or given in return for a service performed, such as the capture of a criminal

Confederacy the 11 southern states that left the United States to form the Confederate States of America during the Civil War

crow's nest lookout post located high above a ship

foreman worker who supervises and directs other workers

gangplank plank used for getting on and off a boat or ship

helm wheel or handle used to steer a boat

navigate steer a course

rigger someone who outfits a ship with rigging, the ropes and chains that hold sails and masts

secede formally withdraw from a group or an organization, often to form another organization

segregation practice of keeping groups of people apart, especially based on race

slavery ownership of other people; slaves are forced to work without pay

stevedore someone who loads and unloads ships at a port

wharf level area built onto a harbour to which a ship can be moored to load and unload

Index

Africa 5
Anti-Slavery Society 57

Castle Pinckney 43
casualties 9
Civil War 5, 8–9, 10, 28
Confederate States of America 8, 28, 30–31, 32, 34, 42–43, 50, 52
crew members 4, 30, 34, 36, 40, 42, 52
crops 6, 11, 14

Douglass, Frederick 15

equal rights 59

Fort Johnson 43
Fort Ripley 43
Fort Sumter 28, 38, 42–43, 45, 46

legal rights 6
Lincoln, Abraham 27, 28, 52, 55

northern states 5, 6, 9, 15, 26

protests 57

Simmons, John 19, 20
slavery 4–5, 6, 10–11, 12, 16, 25, 26–27, 28, 36, 55, 56–57

Smalls, Robert 4, 10, 15, 16–17, 28, 34, 36, 38–39, 40, 42–43, 44–45, 48–49, 50, 52, 55, 56–57, 59

    birth 10

    childhood 12, 18

    death 59

    family 4, 10–11, 12, 14, 24–25, 29, 32, 36, 42, 45, 49, 55

    jobs 16–17, 18, 19, 20, 22, 30–31, 52

soldiers 9, 30, 31, 34, 46, 50, 55

southern states 5, 6, 8–9, 26

Union, the 8, 28, 32, 34, 36, 38–39, 42, 46, 48, 50, 52, 55, 56–57

United States 5, 6, 8, 27

    Georgia 20

    Pennsylvania 57

    South Carolina 4, 10, 16, 18–19, 20, 26, 28, 30–31, 32, 34, 36, 38, 40, 52, 57, 59

US Congress 59